Kids' KNITTED HATS

Knitting hats for children has never been so easy. Our aim, when designing and writing our diagrams and instructions, is to provide you with an understanding of the concept or approach so that you can make you own unique hats. In these hat designs, Deb, Lynda, and fellow designers Dana Gibbons, Megan Lacey, Bernice Vollick and Anne Russell have followed the Cabin Fever creed of minimal finishing. When you are finished knitting, you are finished with the project. So grab your circular needles and enjoy creating hats your little ones will love to wear.

Deb and Linda Gemmell from Cabin Fever

CONTENTS

THE BASICS

KNITTING IN THE ROUND

Using a circular needle, cast on all stitches as instructed. Untwist and straighten on the needle before beginning the first round. Place a marker after the last stitch to mark the beginning of a round. Hold the needle so that the ball of yarn is attached to the stitch closest to the right hand point. To begin working in the round, knit the stitches on the left hand point (Fig. 1).

Continue working each round as instructed without turning the work. After the first round, check to be sure that the cast on edge has not been twisted. If it has been, the only way to correct the twist is to rip out the first round back to the cast row. Join, being careful not to twist the cast on row, and work the first row again. Check again to ensure that the work has not been twisted.

When working a project that is too small to use a circular needle, or the size circular needle is unavailable in the length needed, double pointed needles are required. Divide the number of cast on stitches into thirds or fourths and slip ⅓ or ¼ of the stitches onto each of the double pointed needles forming a triangle or square. With the last needle, knit across the first needle (Fig. 2a – 2b). You will now have an empty needle with which to knit the stitches from the next needle. Work the first stitch of each needle firmly to prevent gaps.

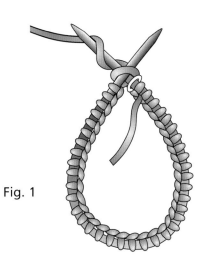

Fig. 1

USING MARKERS
Markers are used to help distinguish the beginning of each round being worked. Use a plastic ring marker or place a 2" (5 cm) scrap piece of yarn before the first stitch of each round, moving the marker after each round is complete.

Fig. 2a

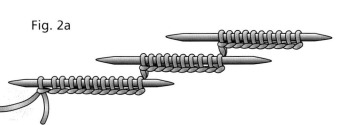

Fig. 2b

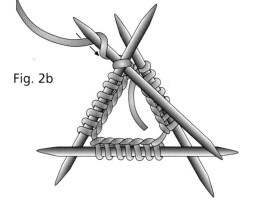

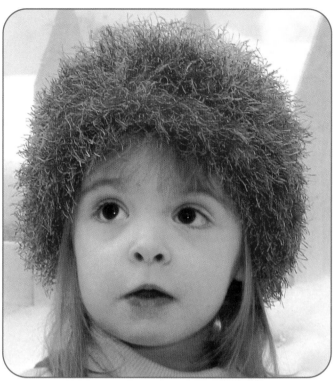

FAUX FUR FUN

Use soft, colorful eyelash yarn in combination with other yarns to create this charming faux fur trimmed hat.

Design by Dana Gibbons
Experience Level: Beginner

SIZES
Finished Circumference: 16-17 (18-20)"

MATERIALS
Heavy Worsted Weight Yarn (Fur)
    Multicolor (A) 1.5 ounces/57 yards, 40 grams/52 meters
Medium Worsted Weight Yarn
    Orange (B) 3.5 ounces/207 yards, 100 grams/
       188 meters
Size 8 (5 mm) 16" (40 cm) circular needle or size to obtain
    gauge
Set of size 8 (5 mm) double pointed needles
Ring marker
Tapestry needle

GAUGE
18 sts = 4" (10 cm)

NOTE: To get the fluffiest effect, the purl side will be used as the right side. But to make the working of the hat easier we will KNIT the Fur section and then turn the hat inside out so that the purl side is showing.

TO BEGIN
With circular needle and color A, cast on 72 (80) sts loosely. Join in the round, being careful not to twist the stitches. Place a marker for the beginning of the round.
Work (K2, P2) rib for 6 rounds.
Knit every round for 3½ (4½)"/9 (11.5) cm.
Cut Color A and turn the hat inside out by pushing your knitting through the center of the circular needle so that now the purl side of the hat is on the outside.

CROWN
Change to double pointed needles when necessary.
Join Color B and knit 1 round.

Large Size ONLY:
Next Round: *K8, K2tog; repeat from * to end of round — 72 sts.
Knit 1 round.

All Sizes:
Decrease Round: *K7, K2tog; repeat from * to end of round — 64 sts.

Knit 1 round.
Decrease Round: *K6, K2tog; repeat from * to end of round — 56 sts.
Knit 1 round.
Decrease Round: *K5, K2tog; repeat from * to end of round — 48 sts.
Knit 1 round.
Decrease Round: *K4, K2tog; repeat from * to end of round — 40 sts.
Knit 1 round.
Decrease Round: *K3, K2tog; repeat from * to end of round — 32 sts.
Knit 1 round.
Decrease Round: *K2, K2tog; repeat from * to end of round — 24 sts.
Knit 1 round.
Decrease Round: *K1, K2tog; repeat from * to end of round — 16 sts.
Knit 1 round.
Next Round: (K2tog) to end of round — 8 sts.
Next Round: (K2tog) to end of round – 4 sts.
Place all stitches on 1 double pointed needle.
Work I-Cord for 4 rounds. See instructions below.
Next Round: While still working the I-Cord technique, K2tog twice — 2 sts.
Next Round: K2tog and fasten off.

I-CORD
Use double pointed needles. Knit 4 sts. *Slide 4 sts to other end of needle. Knit 4 sts (on first stitch pull yarn from last stitch up to first stitch and knit tightly); repeat from * for desired length.

TASSEL
Wrap yarn 25 times around a piece of cardboard 3"/ 7.5cm wide and 3"/ 7.5cm long, break yarn. Thread another piece of yarn through a tapestry needle and wrap around top of yarn on cardboard a few times, tie a knot tightly and break yarn. Cut through wrapped yarn at opposite end from knot. Tightly wrap another strand of yarn 1"/2.5cm down from knotted end to secure the tassel. Trim tassel to even the ends.

CHAMELEON

Whether using silky eyelash or traditional worsted weight yarns, this simple cap will become a unique all-time favorite.

Design by Lynda Gemmell
Experience Level: Beginner

SIZE
To fit Child: 1-2 (3-4, 5-6) years
Finished Circumference: 17 (18, 19)"

MATERIALS
Heavy Worsted Weight Yarn (Fur)
 Multicolor 3 ounces/114 yards, 80 grams/108 meters
OR
Medium Worsted Weight Yarn Orange 3.5 ounces/207 yards, 100 grams/188 meters
Size 8 (5 mm) 16" (40 cm) circular needle or size to obtain gauge
Set of size 8 (5 mm) double pointed needles
Tapestry needle

GAUGE
16 sts = 4" (10 cm)

STARTING AT THE BRIM
With the circular needle, cast on 68 (72, 76) sts. Place marker and join in the round, being careful not to twist stitches.
Knit every round for 5 (5¾, 6)"/13 (14.5, 15.5) cm.

CROWN
Large size ONLY
Decrease Round: *K17, K2tog; repeat from * to end of round — 72 sts.
Next Round: Knit.

All Sizes
Change to double pointed needles when necessary.
Round 1: *K15 (7, 7), K2tog; repeat from * to end of round — 64 sts (all sizes).
Round 2 and Alternate Rounds; Knit.
Round 3: *K6, K2tog; repeat from * to end of round — 56 sts (all sizes).

Round 5: *K5, K2tog; repeat from * to end of round — 48 sts (all sizes).

Round 7: *K4, K2tog; repeat from * to end of round — 40 sts (all sizes).

Round 9: *K3, K2tog; repeat from * to end of round — 32 sts (all sizes).

Round 11: *K2, K2tog; repeat from * to end of round — 24 sts (all sizes).

Round 13: *K1, K2tog; repeat from * to end of round —16 sts (all sizes).

Round 15: *K2tog; repeat from * to end of round — 8 sts (all sizes).

Round 17: *K2tog; repeat from * to end of round — 4 sts (all sizes).

FINISHING

Cut yarn leaving a tail of approximately 6" (15.5 cm). Using a tapestry needle, thread through all the remaining stitches. Pull them tight and secure. Sew in the ends. The end from the cast on round should be sewn in on the Right Side, so that when the brim is rolled up, it does not show.

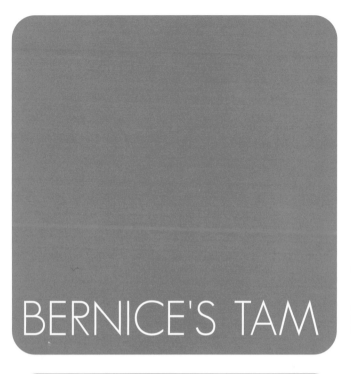

BERNICE'S TAM

Your little one will feel so grown up in this pretty tam. Come chilly weather, she will be warm and stylish.

Designed by Bernice Vollick
Experience Level: Beginner / Intermediate

SIZE
To fit Child: 2 (4) years

MATERIALS
DK, Light Worsted Weight Yarn
    Turquoise 2.5 ounces/168 yards, 70 grams/154 meters
Size 3 (3.25 mm) 16" (40 cm) circular needle
Size 4 (3.5 mm) 16" (40 cm) circular needle or size to
    obtain gauge
Set of size 4 (3.5 mm) double pointed needles
Markers
Tapestry needle

GAUGE
24 sts = 4" (10 cm) with size 4 (3.5 mm) needle

ABBREVIATIONS

YO: Yarn over – bring yarn under right needle to front of work, swing over the right needle to the back of work, ready to work next stitch.

M1: Make one stitch – with left needle lift the running thread between the stitch just worked and the next stitch, from front to back, and knit into the back of the resulting loop.

EYELET PATTERN

Round 1: Purl.
Round 2: Work (K2tog, YO) to end of round.
Round 3: Purl (purl into YO without twisting it to maintain the eyelet).
Round 4: Knit.

TO BEGIN

With smaller circular needle, cast on 96 (104) sts.
Join in the round, being careful not to twist stitches, place marker at beginning of the round.
NOTE: You may want to distinguish the "beginning of the round" marker in some way from the other markers needed further on in the pattern (use a different color or tie a piece of yarn to the marker).
Work (K2, P2) for 1¼" (3 cm).
Next Round: With larger circular needle, knit.

Work Eyelet Pattern once.

INCREASING

Round 1: Slip marker, K12 (13), M1, *Place marker, K12 (13), M1; repeat from * to end of round — 104 (112) sts.
Round 2: Knit.
Round 3: *Slip marker, knit to marker, M1; repeat from * to end of round.
Round 4: Knit.
Repeat last 2 rounds (Rounds 3 & 4) until there are 20 (22) sts between each marker — 160 (176) sts.

Work Eyelet Pattern once.
NOTE: While working the Eyelet Pattern be sure to keep the markers in place.

DECREASING FOR CROWN

Change to double pointed needles when needed.
Round 1: *Slip marker, knit to 2 sts before next marker, K2tog; repeat from * to end of round.
Round 2: Knit.
Repeat last 2 rounds until 32 sts remain on needles, ending with a knit row.
Next Round: Work (K2tog) to end of round — 16 sts.
Next Round: Knit.
Next Round: Work (K2tog) to end of round — 8 sts.

FINISHING

I-CORD Tail (First Option)

Round 1: Knit — 8 sts.
Round 2: (K2tog) 4 times — 4 sts.
Work I-Cord on 4 stitches for 1½" (4 cm). See instructions below. Bind off 4 sts. Break yarn and sew in the ends.

Flat Top (Second Option)

Break yarn leaving about 6"/15 cm of yarn. Thread yarn through remaining 8 sts, pull opening closed and anchor end to the inside of the hat. You could add a pom-pom to the top.

I-CORD

Use double pointed needles. Knit 4 sts. *Slide 4 sts to other end of needle. Knit 4 sts (on first stitch pull yarn from last stitch up to first stitch and knit tightly); repeat from * for desired length.

HALTON CROWN HAT

Children will love wearing this colorful hat with its fun jingle bells, and you will always know where to find them.

Design by Megan Lacey
Experience Level: Intermediate

SIZES

To fit Child: 2 (4, 6) years
Finished Circumference: 17 (18, 19)"

MATERIALS

DK, Light Worsted Weight Yarn approx. 2.5 ounces/
    168 yards, 70 grams/154 meters of each: Blue (A),
    Lime Green (B), Yellow (C), Turquoise (D)
Size 3 (3.25 mm) 16" (40 cm) circular needle or size to
    obtain gauge
Set of size 6 (4 mm) double pointed needles (**NOTE**: For
    binding off only)
4 bells
Marker

GAUGE

24 sts = 4" (10 cm) on size 3 (3.25 mm) needle

HAT

With circular needle and Color A, cast on 102
(108, 114) sts. Mark the beginning of the round.
Join in the round, being careful not to twist your stitches.
Work (K1, P1) rib for 2" (5 cm).

Work Chart.

CROWN

Continue with Color A, knit every round for 2 (2½, 2½)"/
5 (6, 6 cm).

TO FINISH

Next Round: Continue with Color A, knit increasing 2 (4,
6) sts evenly around — 104 (112, 120) sts.
Use the 3-Needle Bind Off to make 4 points on top of hat
as follows:
Using double pointed needles, knit first 13 (14, 15) sts
onto a double pointed needle, knit next 13 (14, 15) sts
onto a second double pointed needle. Work 3-Needle Bind
Off with wrong sides facing (working a ridge on the right
side of hat), until you bind off all stitches. Break yarn.
Reattach yarn and repeat for next point, continuing until
all 4 points are completed. See instructions below.
Attach a bell to each point.

3-NEEDLE BIND OFF

With stitches of Back of hat on 1 needle and stitches
of Front on another, hold Front and Back together
with Wrong Sides facing to make a ridged seam on
the outside (right side) of the hat.
With another (3rd) LARGER sized needle:
1) Insert 3rd needle into first stitch on Front left needle
and, without removing it, insert 3rd needle into first
stitch on Back needle and knit these two stitches
together.
2) Repeat once more.
3) There are 2 stitches on right needle, pass first stitch
over second stitch and off end of needle (the same as
a regular bind off).
Repeat steps 1 and 3 until all the stitches are bind off.

CHART

6	5	4	3	2	1	Row
□	□	○	□	□	○	28
□	○	□	○	□	□	27
○	□	□	□	○	□	26
□	□	○	○	□	□	25
○	○	○	○	○	○	24
✓	✓	✓	✓	✓	✓	23
○	✓	○	✓	○	✓	22
✓	✓	✓	✓	✓	✓	21
□	□	□	□	□	□	20
□	●	□	□	●	□	19
●	●	●	□	□	□	18
●	□	●	●	□	●	17
□	□	●	●	●	●	16
●	□	●	●	□	●	15
●	●	●	□	□	□	14
□	●	□	□	●	□	13
□	□	□	□	□	□	12
✓	✓	✓	✓	✓	✓	11
○	✓	○	✓	○	✓	10
✓	✓	✓	✓	✓	✓	9
●	●	●	●	●	●	8
□	●	□	●	●	●	7
●	□	●	●	□	●	6
□	●	□	●	●	●	5
●	●	●	●	●	●	4
✓	✓	✓	✓	✓	✓	3
○	✓	○	✓	○	✓	2
✓	✓	✓	✓	✓	✓	1

Symbol	Color
□	Blue
●	Lime Green
○	Yellow
✓	Turquoise

Left: Here Kitty
Right: Blue & White

BLUE & WHITE

This cute and comfy patterned hat is easy to knit and can be stitched in the traditional blue and white, as shown, or in the child's favorite colors.

Design by Bernice Vollick
Experience Level: Intermediate

SIZES
To fit Child: 2 (4-6) years
Finished Circumference: 17 (19)"

MATERIALS
Medium Worsted Weight Yarn
    (Strong contrast in the colors works best, e.g.
        Royal/Cream; Deep Purple/Pale Gold; Black/
        White; Red/White.)
    Periwinkle (MC) 5 ounces/236 yards, 140 grams/
        212 meters
    White (CC) 5 ounces/236 yards, 140 grams/212 meters
4 markers (use a different color marker for the beginning
    of the round)
Size 7 (4.5 mm) 16" (40 cm) circular needle or size to
    obtain gauge
Set of size 7 (4.5 mm) double pointed needles

GAUGE
16 stitches = 4" (10 cm)

ABBREVIATIONS
K2tog: Knit 2 stitches together
SSK (Slip 1, Slip1, Knit 2 together): Slip stitch as if to
knit, slip next stitch as if to knit, insert left needle into
front of 2 slipped stitches on right needle and knit 2
together – decreases 1 st.

TO BEGIN
With circular needle and MC, cast on 68 (76) stitches.
Join in a circle, being careful not to twist stitches.
Place marker at beginning of round.
Knit 8 rounds.
Work (K2, P2) ribbing for 4 rounds.
Knit 1 round, increasing 4 sts evenly — 72 (80) sts.
Purl 1 round.
Work Chart.
Break CC yarn.
With MC, knit 1 round.

RIDGE
Purl 3 rounds.

DECREASING FOR CROWN
Change to double pointed needles when necessary.

Set-Up Round: *K18 (20), place marker; repeat from * to
end of round.
Round 1: *K2tog, knit to 2 stitches before marker, SSK,
slip marker; repeat from * to end of round — 64 (72) sts.
Round 2: Knit.
Repeat last two rounds until 32 stitches remain on the
needles, ending with a knit round.
Next Round: Work (K2tog) to end of round — 16 sts.
Next Round: Knit
Next Round: Work (K2tog) to end of round — 8 sts.

FINISHING
Break yarn, thread yarn through remaining 8 stitches, pull
opening closed, take yarn to wrong side and anchor end
of thread.

Optional Embellishments
Attach choice of: pom-pom, tassel, decorative button, bell,
etc. to the center of the top of hat.

CHART

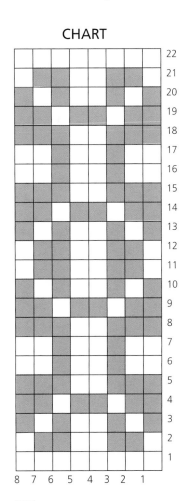

☐ CC – Contrast Color
▨ MC – Main Color

*Read all rounds
  from left to right

HERE KITTY

Why wait 'til halloween to dress up like a kitty! This cute cat hat is fun to wear every day.

Designed by Dana Gibbons
Experience Level: Beginner-Intermediate

SIZES
To fit Child: 1-3 years
Finished Circumference: 17½"

MATERIALS
DK, Light Worsted Weight Yarn
    Royal Blue 2.5 ounces/168 yards, 70 grams/154 meters
Size 5 (3.75 mm) 16" (40 cm) circular needle or size to
    obtain gauge.
Set of size 5 (3.75 mm) double pointed needles
3 markers

GAUGE
22 sts = 4" (10 cm)

ABBREVIATIONS
K2tog: Knit 2 stitches together.
M1: Make one stitch – with left needle lift the running thread between the stitch just worked and the next stitch, from front to back, and knit into the back of the resulting loop.
SSK (Slip 1, Slip1, Knit 2 together): Slip stitch as if to knit, slip next stitch as if to knit, insert left needle into front of 2 slipped stitches on right needle and knit 2 together – decreases 1 st.

TO BEGIN
With circular needle, cast on 96 sts.
Join in the round, being careful not to twist your stitches, place marker.
Work (K1, P1) rib for 1" (2.5 cm)

BODY
Knit every round for 3" (7.5 cm).

EARS
Set-Up Round: K24, place marker, K48, place marker, knit to end of round.
NOTE: You may wish to make the "beginning of round" marker different in some way; use a different color or tie a piece of brightly colored yarn to it.
Increase Round: *Knit to 1 stitch before marker, M1, K1, slip marker, K1, M1; repeat from * once more, knit to end of round — 100 sts.
Next Round: Knit.
Repeat last 2 rounds 6 more times — 124 sts.
Decrease Round: *Knit to 2 sts before marker, SSK, slip marker, K2tog; repeat from * once more, knit to end of round — 120 sts.

BIND OFF
Set-Up: With a double pointed needle, K30. Drop yarn. leave next 60 sts on circular needle. Slip the last 30 sts onto a second double needle pointed needle.
NOTE: You now have half of the stitches (60 sts) on the circular needle for the Front of the hat. One quarter of the stitches (30 sts) on a double pointed needle and the other quarter of the stitches (30 sts) on a second double pointed needle for the back of the hat. The working yarn is at the ear tip.
With right sides facing each other, Bind Off using 3-needle bind off method, working from ear tip to ear tip. Weave in ends.

Left: Here Kitty
Right: Blue & White

3-NEEDLE BIND OFF

With stitches of Back of hat on 1 needle and stitches of Front on another, hold Front and Back together with Wrong Sides facing to make a ridged seam on the outside (right side) of the hat.

With another (3rd) LARGER sized needle:

1) Insert 3rd needle into first stitch on Front left needle and, without removing it, insert 3rd needle into first stitch on Back needle and knit these two stitches together.

2) Repeat once more.

3) There are 2 stitches on right needle, pass first stitch over second stitch and off end of needle (the same as a regular bind off).

Repeat steps 1 and 3 until all the stitches are bind off.

TAIL

With a double pointed needle, pick up 4 sts at the center Back of the cast on edge of the hat.

Work 4-stitch I-Cord for 4" (10 cm).

Optional Embellishments

You can embroider a face and/or nose on the Front of the hat, or add bells or tassels to the ear tips.

I-CORD

Use double pointed needles. Knit 4 sts. *Slide 4 sts to other end of needle. Knit 4 sts (on first stitch pull yarn from last stitch up to first stitch and knit tightly); repeat from * for desired length.

JUMPING JACKS

This playful hat is a fun addition to your child's winter wardrobe. What mother or grandmother wouldn't love making several for their little darlings?

Design by Anne Russell
Experience Level: Intermediate

SIZES
To fit Child: 1-3 (4-8) years
Finished Circumference: 17 (20)"

MATERIALS
DK, Light Worsted Weight Yarn
 Black (Dark) 5 ounces/459 yards, 141 grams/
  336 meters
 Aqua (Light) 5 ounces/459 yards, 141 grams/
  336 meters
Size 6 (4 mm) 16" (40 cm) circular needle or size to
 obtain gauge
Set of size 6 (4 mm) double pointed needles

GAUGE
24 sts = 4" (10 cm)

ABBREVIATIONS
K2tog: Knit 2 together.
SL1: Slip 1.
Psso: Pass slipped stitch over.

CORRUGATED RIBBING (Variation of K2, P2 ribbing)
Set-Up Round: *With Dark color K2, with Light color K2;
repeat from * to end of round.
Rib Round: *With Dark color K2, bring Light color yarn to
front, P2, move Light color to back; repeat from * to end
of round, stranding yarn not in use across back of work
loosely.
Repeat Rib Round.

TO BEGIN
With Dark color, cast on 104 (120) sts. Join in round, being
careful not to twist your stitches and place marker for
beginning of round.
Purl 1 round.
Work in Corrugated Ribbing for 1".

BODY
Small Size ONLY:
Next Round: With Dark color, knit, increasing 1 stitch —
105 sts.
Work Chart B (next page); the pattern repeats 7 times
around the hat.
Next Round: With Dark color, knit.

Large Size ONLY:
The large size includes 2 "Peerie" patterns (Chart A) which
give extra height to accommodate an older child.
Next Round: With Dark color, knit.
Work Chart A; the pattern repeats 24 times around the
hat. 6 = 7N1
Work Chart B; the pattern repeats 8 times around the
hat. 18 = 7N 7N1 7N1 7N
Work Chart A; the pattern repeats 24 times around the
hat. 6 = 7N
Next Round: With Dark color, knit.

CROWN All Sizes
Work Chart C. Where indicated on the chart, work
decreases by SL1, K1, Psso at beginning of repeat and
K2tog at end of repeat. On last row of chart, work
decreases by SL1, K2tog, Psso — 7 (8) sts.

FINISHING
I-Cord Tail (First Option)
Small: With Dark color, (K2tog) 3 times, K1 — 4 sts.
Large: With Dark color, (K2tog) 4 times — 4 sts.
All Sizes: With Dark color, Knit I-Cord for 2".
Next Round: (K2tog) twice — 2 sts.
Next Round: K2tog, pull yarn through and fasten off.
Tie the I-cord in a knot on top.

Flat Crown (Second Option)
Break yarn and thread through remaining stitches, draw
tight and secure.

JUMPING JACKS CHARTS

CHART A

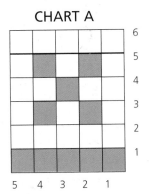

Dark Color
Light Color

CHART B

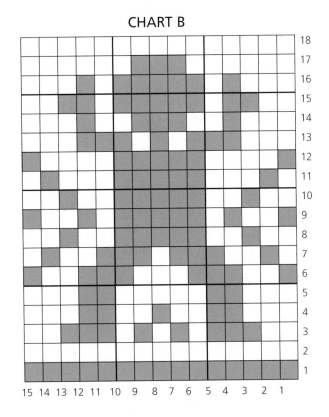

CHART C

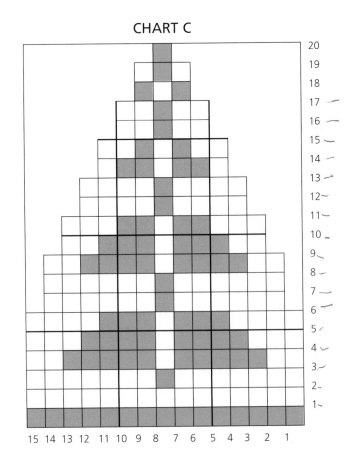

LITTLE FLAP-CAP

When the wind blows and Jack Frost is in the air, this cozy cap will keep little ears toasty warm. The colorful decorative border pattern adds interest to this very functional cap.

Design by Lynda Gemmell
Experience Level: Intermediate

For the sizing of this hat, we used two different weights of yarn. The pattern has a small and large size. If knit in worsted weight yarn the small and large sizes will result in a newborn and 2-year-old size. If the same small and large sizes are knit in chunky weight yarn the resulting hat will fit 4- and 6-year-olds. Check material and needle sizes carefully for your size.

SIZE
To fit Child: newborn (2, 4, 6) years.
Finished Circumference: 14 (16, 18, 19½)"

MATERIALS
For newborn & 2 years:
Medium Worsted Weight Yarn:
    Red speckled (MC) 3 ounces/197 yards,
       85 grams/180 meters
    Blue (CC 1) approximately 20 yards

Yellow (CC 2) approximately 35 yards
Size 7 (4.5 mm) 16" (40 cm) circular needle or size to
    obtain gauge
Set of size 7 (4.5 mm) double pointed needles

For Sizes 4- & 6-year-old:
Chunky Weight Yarn 3 ounces/135 yards (859/125 M):
    Red (MC) – 1 ball
    Blue (CC 1) – 1 ball
    Yellow (CC 2) – 1 ball
Sizes 9 (5.5 mm) 16" (40 cm) circular needle or size
    to obtain gauge
Set of size 9 (5.5 mm) double pointed needles

GAUGE

20 sts = 4" (10 cm) with worsted weight yarn on size 7
    (4.5 mm) needle.
16 sts = 4" (10 cm) with bulky weight yarn on size 9
    (5.5 mm) needle

ABBREVIATIONS

K2tog: Knit 2 stitches together.
M1: Make one stitch – with left needle lift the running
thread between the stitch just worked and the next stitch,
from front to back, and knit into the back of the resulting
loop.

STARTING AT THE BACK — THE EAR FLAP

With Main Color (MC) and circular needle, cast on 40 sts.
Knit 9 rows in garter stitch (knit every row working back
and forth on circular needle).

SHAPE EAR FLAP

Each side of the ear flap is shaped separately using short
rows. These rows are so named because you will only work
across part of the row of knitting, then you will turn your
work and knit back to the beginning of the row. It will
look a little strange for awhile, but hang in there!

NOTE: Using the Wrap & TURN prevents holes from forming when working the following short rows.

WRAP & TURN: Slip the next stitch onto the right
needle, bring yarn forward and, leaving the yarn at the
front of work, slip the stitch back onto the left needle,
TURN.

Short Row 1: K19, Wrap & TURN; knit back to beginning
of row.
Short Row 2: K17, Wrap & TURN; knit back to beginning
of row.
Short Row 3: K15, Wrap & TURN; knit back to beginning
of row.
Short Row 4: K13, Wrap & TURN; knit back to beginning
of row.
Short Row 5: K11, Wrap & TURN; knit back to beginning
of row.
Short Row 6: K9, Wrap & TURN; knit back to beginning
of row.
Short Row 7: K7, Wrap & TURN; knit back to beginning
of row.
Next Row: Knit across the entire row.

Shape the other side of the ear flap: Repeat Rows 1-7,
turning and knitting back. Be sure to knit across the entire
row at the end.

BODY

In the next round you will increase some stitches at the
back of the neck, cast on stitches for the forehead and join
the stitches in the round. The hat can then be worked in
the round.

Round 1: Knit 17, (M1, K1) 6 times, K17, cast on 26 (32)
sts for forehead.
You should have a total of 72 (78) stitches on your needle.
Join in the round, being careful not to twist the stitches.
Work to center back of flap: P5, K18, place marker.
ALL ROUNDS now begin at the center back of hat.
Next Round: K18, P36 (42), K18.
Next Round: Knit.
Next Round: Knit 18, P36 (42), knit to marker.
Next Round: Knit.

CHART

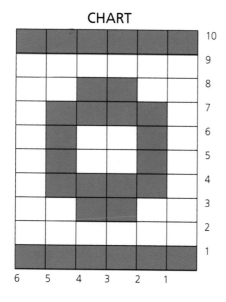

10
9
8
7
6
5
4
3
2
1

6 5 4 3 2 1

CC 1 – Contrast Color 1
CC 2 – Contrast Color 2

*Read each round from right to left

Work the Color Pattern Chart.

CROWN

With MC, **knit every round** until your work measures approximately 3¼ (3½)"/8 (9) cm from the 2nd cast on edge at the forehead.
Begin decreasing as follows:

Large size ONLY:

Next Round: *K11, K2tog; repeat from * to end of round — 72 sts.
Next Round: Knit.

All sizes: (72 sts on needle)

Round 1: *K10, K2tog; repeat from * to end of round — 66 sts.
Round 2 and all alternate Rounds: knit.

Round 3: *K9, K2tog; repeat from * to end of round — 60 sts.
Round 5: *K8, K2tog; repeat from * to end of round — 54 sts.
Round 7: *K7, K2tog; repeat from * to end of round — 48 sts.
Round 9: *K6, K2tog; repeat from * to end of round — 42 sts.
Continue to decrease every other round, knitting one less stitch between decreases until 12 sts remain on needles.
Next Round: *K2, K2tog; repeat from * to end of round — 9 sts.

FINISHING

Three I-Cord Tails (First Option)

Divide the 9 sts onto 3 double point needles.
With MC, work I-Cord (see below) on 3 sts on double point needle until the tail measures approximately 2"/5 cm. Bind off and sew in ends. With CC 1, knit next 3 sts on double point needle, work 3-stitch I-Cord as above. Work last 3 sts with CC 2 as above.

Pointy Tip (Second Option)

Break the yarn, leaving approximately 6"/15 cm of yarn. Using a tapestry needle, thread tail of yarn through the remaining stitches and pull tightly to close the top of the hat. Secure firmly.

Tie Ups

The ties may be knit in the MC or in one or more of the CC. Pick up 3 stitches from the inside edge of the front corner of the ear flap and work I-Cord for 10"/25.5 cm or to desired length. Make a second tie.

I-CORD
Use 2 double pointed needles. Knit 3 sts. *Slide 3 sts to other end of the needle. Knit 3 sts (on first stitch, pull yarn from last stitch up to the first stitch and knit tightly); repeat from * for desired length.

CANDY DOTS

This colorful pillbox hat uses slip stitches to create the look of candy dots. It will delight children everywhere.

Design by Dana Gibbons
Experience Level: Intermediate

SIZES
Finished Circumference: 16 (18, 20)"

MATERIALS
Worsted Weight Yarn
  White (A) 4 ounces/189 yards, 113 grams/172 meters
  Periwinkle (B) 4 ounces/189 yards, 113 grams/
    172 meters
  Multicolor (C) 4 ounces/ 189 yards, 113 grams/
    172 meters
Size 5 (3.75 mm) 16" (40 cm) circular needle
Size 7 (4.5 mm) 16" (40 cm) circular needle or size to
    obtain gauge
Set of size 7 (4.5 mm) double pointed needles
Ring marker

GAUGE
20 sts = 4" (10 cm) with size 7 (4.5 mm) needle

ABBREVIATIONS
wyib: With yarn in back of work.
SL1(p): Slip one stitch purlwise.

NOTE: The rolled ridges are added after the hat is completed.

SLIP STITCH PATTERN
Round 1: With Color C, *wyib SL1(p), K1; repeat from * to end of round.
Round 2: With Color C, *wyib SL1(p), P1; repeat from * to end of round.
Rounds 3 & 4: With Color A, knit.

TO BEGIN
With smaller circular needle and Color A, cast on 80 (88, 96) sts.
Join in the round, being careful not to twist your stitches, place marker.
Work (K1, P1) rib for 1" (2.5 cm).
Change to larger circular needle.
Rounds 1 & 2: With Color A, knit. Drop Color A.
Round 3: With Color B, knit.
Ridge Round 4: With Color B, purl. Cut Color B.
Rounds 5 & 6: With Color A, knit.

Work Slip Stitch Pattern for 4 (4, 4½)"/10 (10, 11) cm. Cut Color C.
Next Round: With Color B, knit.
Ridge Round: With Color B, purl. Cut Color B.

CROWN
Change to double pointed needles when necessary.
Decrease Round: With Color A *K8 (9, 10), K2tog; repeat from * to end of round — 72 (80, 88) sts.
Knit 1 round.
Decrease Round: *K7 (8, 9), K2tog; repeat from * to end of round.
Knit 1 round.
Decrease Round: *K6 (7, 8), K2tog; repeat from * to end of round.
Knit 1 round.
Continue to work decrease round and knit rounds, knitting one stitch less between decreases as set, until there are 16 sts on needles.
Next Round: Work K2tog to end of round — 8 sts.
Cut cotton leaving an 8" (20 cm) tail. Thread yarn tail through loops on needles and pull tight and secure.

RIDGES
Top Ridge: With Color B and larger circular needle, pick up and knit 1 stitch for every purl stitch of ridge; insert needle into the top of the purl stitch to pick up stitch — 80 (88, 96) sts. Place marker.
Knit 3 rounds.
Bind Off knitwise. Ridge will curl naturally.
Repeat as above for bottom ridge. Weave in ends.

CABLE RIB HAT

By combining decorative cables and fun yarns, you can create this interesting pillbox style cap. It's great to wear on those chilly days when kids love to play outdoors.

Designed by Megan Lacey
Experience Level: Intermediate

SIZES

To fit Child: 1 (2-6) years
Finished Circumference: 16 (18)"

MATERIALS

Medium Worsted Weight Yarn
   Red speckled 3 ounces/197 yards, 85 grams/180 meters
Size 7 (4.5 mm) 16" (40 cm) circular needle or size to
   obtain gauge
Set of size 7 (4.5 mm) double pointed needles
Cable Needle

GAUGE

22 sts = 4" (10 cm)

ABBREVIATION

T2L (Twist 2 Left): Slip next stitch onto a cable needle and hold at front of work, purl next stitch from left needle, knit into back of stitch on cable needle.

> **CABLE RIB PATTERN:**
> **Round 1:** *(K1, P1) twice, K2, P1; repeat from * to end of round.
> **Round 2:** Repeat Row 1.
> **Round 3:** *P1, K1, P2, T2L, P1; repeat from * to end of round.
> **Round 4:** *P1, K1, P2, K2, P1; repeat from * to end of round.
> **Round 5:** *(K1, P1) twice, T2L, P1; repeat from * to end of round.

HAT

With circular needle, cast on 91 (98) sts. Join in the round, being careful not to twist stitches.
Purl 3 rounds.
Work Rounds 1-5 of Cable Rib Pattern once.
Repeat Rounds 2-5 of Cable Rib Pattern until hat measures 3½ (4½)"/9 (11.5) cm from cast on edge.
Purl 3 rounds.

SHAPE CROWN

In the next round adjust for the crown:

Set-Up Round: Knit, decreasing 1 st for small size or increase 1 st for larger size — 90 (99 sts).

Next Round: Knit.

Large Size ONLY:

Next Round: (K9, K2tog) 9 times — 90 sts.

Next Round: Knit.

ALL Sizes:

Both sizes of hat now have 90 sts.

Change to double pointed needles when necessary.

Round 1: (K8, K2tog) 9 times — 81 sts.

Round 2 and all alternating rounds: Knit.

Round 3: (K7, K2tog) 9 times — 72 sts.

Round 5: (K6, K2tog) 9 times — 63 sts.

Round 7: (K5, K2tog) 9 times — 54 sts.

Round 9: (K4, K2tog) 9 times — 45 sts.

Round 11: (K3, K2tog) 9 times — 36 sts.

Round 13: (K2, K2tog) 9 times — 27 sts.

Round 15: (K1, K2tog) 9 times — 18 sts.

Round 17: (K2tog) 9 times — 9 sts.

Next Round: Knit. Break yarn and thread tail through the remaining stitches; fasten off and sew to inside of hat.

FINISHING

Sew in all ends.

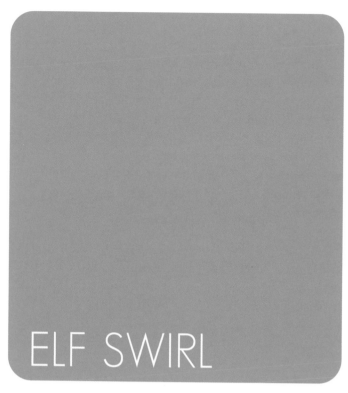

ELF SWIRL

The secret to making this easy cap is in using self-striping wool and the unique pattern. Together they give a colorful, swirling effect to the impish cap.

Design by Deb Gemmell
Experience Level: Beginner

SIZE
To fit Child: 0-2 (4-6) years
Finished Circumference: 16½ (18)"

MATERIALS
Fine/Sport Weight Yarn
    Multicolor 3.5 ounces/330 yards, 100 grams/
      300 meters
Size 4 (3.5 mm) 16" (40 cm) circular needle or size to
    obtain gauge.
Set of size 4 (3.5 mm) double pointed needles
10 markers

GAUGE
24 sts = 4" (10 cm)

ABBREVIATIONS
SSK (Slip 1, Slip1, Knit 2 together): Slip stitch as if to knit, slip next stitch as if to knit, insert left needle into front of 2 slipped stitches on right needle and knit 2 together – decreases 1 st.

SSSK3tog (Slip 3, Knit 3 stitches together): Slip stitch as if to knit, slip next stitch as if to knit, and slip one more stitch as if to knit, insert left needle into front of 3 slipped stitches on right needle and knit 3 together – decreases 2 sts.

YO: Yarn over – bring yarn under right needle to front of work, swing over the right needle to the back of work, ready to work next stitch.

M1: Make one stitch – with left needle lift the running thread between the stitch just worked and the next stitch, from front to back, and knit into the back of the resulting loop.

TO BEGIN
Using the circular needle, cast on 100 (110) sts.
Join in the round, being careful not to twist stitches. Place marker for beginning of round.
Knit every round for 3 (4)"/7.5 (10) cm. (The bottom inch will roll up to form the brim.)
Change to double pointed needles when necessary.
Marker Round: Slip marker, SSK, K8 (9), YO, *place marker, SSK, K8 (9), YO; repeat from * to end of round.
NOTE: You may wish to make the "beginning of round" marker different in some way from the other 9 markers; use a different marker color or tie a piece of brightly colored yarn to the "beginning of round" marker.
Next Round: Knit.

SWIRL
Round 1: *Slip marker, SSK, knit to next marker, YO; repeat from * to end of round.
Round 2: Knit.
Round 3-6: Repeat Rounds 1 & 2 twice.
Round 7-Decrease: *Slip marker, SSSK3tog, knit to next marker, YO; repeat from * to end of round.
Round 8: Knit.
Repeat last 8 rounds until 20 (30) sts remain on the needles.
Next Round: *SSK, M1; repeat from * to end of round.
Repeat last round twice more.
Next Round: Work (SSK) to end of round — 10 (15) sts.
Knit 3 rounds.
Next Round: *SSK; repeat until there are 5 sts remaining on needles — 5 sts).

TUFTED CAST OFF
Last Round: *Cast on 10 sts, bind off 11 sts, slip 1 stitch on right needle back onto left needle; repeat from * to end of round.
Break yarn leaving a 10" (25 cm) tail.
Wrap tail around the base of the tufted ends several times. Sew end through to the inside of the hat and secure.

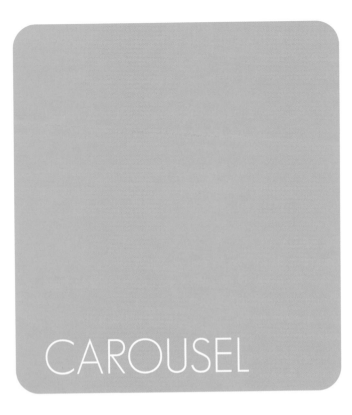

CAROUSEL

Simple patterns, great color and animal charms are used to create this carousel cap. A picot edging completes the project with a touch of whimsy.

Design by Dana Gibbons
Experience Level: Intermediate

SIZES
Finished Circumference: 16 (17-18)"

MATERIALS
DK, Light Worsted Weight Yarn
    Royal Blue (A) 2.5 ounces/168 yards, 70 grams/
       154 meters
    Yellow (B) 2.5 ounces/168 yards, 70 grams/154 meters
    Red (C) 2.5 ounces/168 yards, 70 grams/154 meters
Size 4 (3.5 mm) 16" (40 cm) circular needle
Size 6 (4.0 mm) 16" (40 cm) circular needle or size to
    obtain gauge
Set of size 6 (4.0 mm) double pointed needles
5 markers
6-8 animal buttons

GAUGE
24 sts = 4" (10 cm) with size 6 (4.0 mm) needle

ABBREVIATIONS
K2tog: Knit 2 stitches together.
SL1(p): Slip one stitch purlwise.
SSK (Slip 1, Slip1, Knit 2 together): Slip stitch as if to knit, slip next stitch as if to knit, insert left needle into front of 2 slipped stitches on right needle and knit 2 together – decreases 1 st.
wyib: With yarn in back of work.
YO: Yarn over – bring yarn under right needle to front of work, swing over the right needle to the back of work, ready to work next stitch.

TO BEGIN
With smaller circular needle and Color A, cast on 96 (104) sts. Place marker and join in the round, being careful not to twist stitches.
Work (K1, P1) rib for 1" (2.5 cm).
Drop Color A but do not cut.

PICOT EDGE
Change to larger circular needle.
With Color B, knit 4 rounds.
Picot Round: *YO, K2tog; repeat from * to end of round.
Knit 3 rounds. Cut Color B.

Fold the Color B section in half at the picot round. In the next round the picot edge is attached to itself by knitting together the next round and the first wrong side round of Color B.
Next Round: *Insert tip of right needle into the Color B loop of first round of Color B on the wrong side of hat and lift this stitch onto the left needle, with RIGHT SIDE FACING and with Color A, K2tog (1 stitch from the needle together with the Color B loop); repeat from * to end of round. This folds the picot edge and secures it.

SLIP STITCH RIB
Round 1: With Color C, *K1, wyib SL1(p); repeat from * to end of round.
Round 2: With Color A, *wyib SL1(p), P1; repeat from * to end of round.

Alternative Method:
The above rounds grow slowly. You can also achieve the same effect by using 2 colors in the same round.
Round 1: K1 with Color C, P1 with Color A.
Repeat last round.

BODY

Join in Color C and work Slip Stitch Rib for 3 (3½)"/ 7.5 (8.5) cm. Drop Color C and cut Color A.

PICOT EDGE

With Color B, knit 8 rounds.
Picot Round: *YO, K2tog; repeat from * to end of round.
Knit 7 rounds. Cut Color B.
Fold the Color B section in half at the picot round. In the next round the picot edge is attached to itself by knitting together the next round and the wrong side of the first round of Color B.
Next Round: *Insert tip of right needle into the Color B loop of first round of Color B on the wrong side of hat and lift this stitch onto the left needle, with RIGHT SIDE FACING and with Color C, K2tog (1 stitch from the needle together with the Color B loop); repeat from * to end of round. This folds the picot edge and secures it.

CROWN

Change to double pointed needles when necessary.
Marker Round: With Color C, slip "beginning of round" marker, K12 (13), (place marker, K24 (26)) 3 times, place marker, K12 (13).

NOTE: You may want to make the "beginning of round" marker different in some way from the markers now set for the crown decreases. Use a different marker color or tie a piece of bright colored yarn to it.
Decrease Round: Knit to 3 sts before the marker, *K2tog, K1, slip marker, K1, SSK; repeat from * at next 3 markers, knit to end of round.
Knit 1 round.
Repeat last 2 rounds until there are 16 sts remaining on needles.
Next Round: Removing markers, (K2tog) to end of round — 8 sts. Cut Color C.
With Color A, knit 5 rounds.
Cut yarn leaving an 8" tail. Thread tail through remaining stitches on needles, pull tight and fasten off. Weave in ends.

FINISHING

Sew on buttons, spacing them evenly around the hat and alternating higher and lower as on a carousel.
NOTE: *Please do not use the animal buttons if knitting this cap for a very young child.*

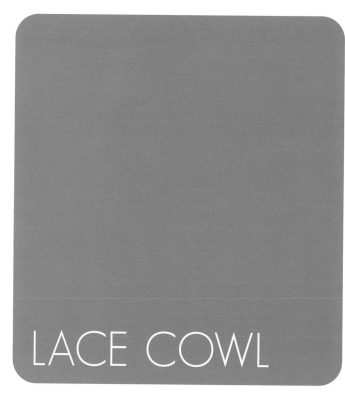

LACE COWL

Keep your child warm and cozy with this lovely lace cowl, which can be worn around the neck or over the head as a hood. The lace provides elasticity so it can be stretched to accommodate various head sizes.

Designed by Lynda Gemmell
Experience Level: Intermediate

SIZES
Circumference before blocking: 16 (17, 18, 19)"

MATERIALS
Light Worsted Weight Yarn
    Aqua 5 ounces/459 yards, 141 grams/420 meters
Size 6 (4 mm) 16" (40 cm) circular needle or size to
    obtain gauge
Marker

GAUGE
Approx. 5 sts = 4" (10 cm) over Lace Pattern

ABBREVIATIONS
K2tog: Knit 2 stitches together.
SL1: Slip 1 stitch.
Psso: Pass slipped stitch over.
YO: Yarn over – bring yarn under right needle to front of work, swing over the right needle to the back of work, ready to work next stitch.

> **LACE PATTERN:**
> **Round 1:** *K2tog, yo, K1, yo, SL1, K1, PSSO; repeat from * to end of round.
> **Round 2:** Knit.

TO BEGIN
Loosely cast on 80 (84, 90, 94) stitches. Place marker and join in the round, being careful not to twist stitches.
Work (K1, P1) rib for 1"(2.5 cm). In last round of ribbing, increase 0 (1, 0, 1) stitch at end of round — 80 (85, 90, 95) sts.
Work the Lace Pattern until cowl measures 11 (12, 13, 13)"/ 28 (30.5, 33, 33) cm from cast on edge.
Work (K1, P1) rib, decreasing 0 (1, 0, 1) stitch at beginning of round — 80 (84, 90, 94) sts.
Work (K1, P1) rib for 1" (2.5 cm).
Bind Off loosely in rib.

REVERSIBLE HAT

This reversible hat looks great with the brim up, brim down, inside or out, because it is completely reversible! It's so much fun to knit, you will want to make several.

Design by Deb Gemmell
Experience Level: Beginner

SIZES
Finished Circumference: 17 (18, 20)"

MATERIALS
Medium Worsted Weight Yarn
   Red 3 ounces/197 yards, 85 grams/189 meters
Size 6 (4 mm) 16" (40 cm) circular needle or size to
   obtain gauge
Set of size 6 (4 mm) double pointed needles
2 markers

GAUGE
20 sts = 4" (10 cm)

ABBREVIATIONS
K2tog: Knit 2 stitches together.
SSK (Slip 1, Slip1, Knit 2 together): Slip stitch as if to knit, slip next stitch as if to knit, insert left needle into front of 2 slipped stitches on right needle and knit 2 together – decreases 1 st.

TO BEGIN
Starting at the bottom edge: 78
With circular needle, cast on 84 (92, 100) sts.
Place marker and join in the round, being careful not to twist stitches.
Round 1: Work (K1, P1) rib to end of round.
Round 2: Knit.
Repeat last 2 rounds until hat measures 4 (5, 6)"/10 (13, 15) cm.

CROWN
Change to double pointed needles when necessary.
Set-Up Round: Remove marker, K1, Replace "beginning of round" marker (all rounds begin here), P1, (K1, P1) 20 (22, 24) times, K1, place second marker, P1, (K1, P1) 20 (22, 24) times, K1.
Decrease Round: *Slip marker, K1, SSK, knit to 2 sts before next marker, K2tog; repeat from * to end of round.
Pattern Round: *Slip marker, P1, K1, work rib as set to 1 stitch before marker, K1; repeat from * to end of round.
Repeat last 2 rounds until 40 (44, 48) sts remain on needle.
Decrease Round 1: *Slip marker, K1, SSK, knit to 2 sts before next marker, K2tog; repeat from * to end of round.
Decrease Round 2: *Slip marker, P1, SSK, work rib as set to 2 sts before next marker, K2tog; repeat from * to end of round.
Repeat last 2 decrease rounds until 8 sts remain on needles. Cut yarn leaving an 8" (20 cm) tail. Thread this tail through the remaining stitches, pull tight and secure.
Sew the tails in carefully so that you can wear the hat with either pattern showing and the brim turned up so the opposite pattern shows.

Left: Reversible Hat
Right: Ribbed Cap

RIBBED CAP

Here's a simple, easy and colorful cap. The rib stitch is very elastic and adjusts to many head sizes which makes them great looking caps for young and old alike.

Design by Deb & Lynda Gemmell
Experience Level: Beginner

SIZES
To fit Child: 1-3 (4-6) years
Finished Circumference: 14-17 (17-21)"

MATERIALS
Medium Worsted Weight Yarn
    Yellow 3 ounces/197 yards, 85 grams/180 meters
    Blue 3 ounces/197 yards, 85 grams/180 meters
Size 7 (4.5 mm) 16" (40 cm) circular needle or size to
    obtain gauge
Set of 5 size 7 (4.5 mm) double pointed needles

GAUGE
25 sts = 4" (10 cm) in Rib Stitch

DOUBLE DECREASE
SL2(k)-K1-Psso: With right needle, slip 2 stitches together knitwise, knit next stitch, pass the 2 slipped stitches over the knit stitch and off the end of the right needle.

TO BEGIN

Using the circular needle, cast on 88 (104) sts.
Place marker and join in the round, being careful not to twist the stitches.
Work in (K1, P1) Rib for 6 (8)"/15 (20) cm.

SHAPE CROWN

Change to double pointed needles when necessary. With a set of 5 double pointed needles, you can center the decrease points in the middle of each of the 4 double pointed needles and then work with the 5th needle.
NOTE: It is important to use the Double Decrease specified in pattern. The SL2(k)-K1-P2sso decrease forms a straight vertical stitch which is essential for the crown formation.
First Decrease Round: Rib across 9 (11) sts, *SL2(k)-K1-P2sso, Rib across 19 (23) sts; repeat from * ending with Rib 10 (12) sts.
Second Decrease Round: Rib across 8 (10) sts, *SL2(k)-K1-P2sso, Rib across 17 (21) sts; repeat from * ending with Rib 9 (11) sts.
Rib Round: Work in (K1, P1) Rib.
NOTE: The (K1, P1) should work perfectly with the stitches of the hat as you work around.
Third Decrease Round: Rib across 7 (9) sts, *SL2(k)-K1-P2sso, Rib across 15 (19) sts; repeat from * ending with Rib 8 (10) sts.
Fourth Decrease Round: Rib across 6 (8) sts, *SL2(k)-K1-P2sso, Rib across 13 (17) sts; repeat from * ending with Rib 7 (9) sts.
Rib Round: Work in (K1, P1) Rib.
Fifth Decrease Round: Rib across 5 (7) sts, *SL2(k)-K1-P2sso, Rib across 11 (15) sts; repeat from * ending with Rib 6 (8) sts.
Sixth Decrease Round: Rib across 4 (6) sts, *SL2(k)-K1-P2sso, Rib across 9 (13) sts; repeat from * ending with Rib 5 (7) sts.
Rib Round: Work in (K1, P1) Rib.
Continue by working 2 Decrease Rounds followed by 1 Rib Round. For each of the Decrease Rounds work 2 less stitches between the 4 decrease points established, until there are 8 sts left on needles. Break the yarn, leaving yourself approximately 6" (15 cm) of yarn. Thread, using a blunt sewing needle, through all the remaining stitches and pull tightly to close the top of the hat. Secure firmly. Turn up the brim and sew the end in so that it doesn't show.

WAVES

Get ready to make waves this winter with this stylish hat. Heads will turn when knitting in either subtle or wild multi-colored yarns to achieve completely different looks.

Design by Deb Gemmell
Experience Level: Enthusiastic Beginner

SIZES
To fit Child: 1-2 (4-6) years
Finished Circumference: 17 (19)"

MATERIALS
Fine/Sport Weight Yarn
    Multicolor – 3.5 ounces/330 yards, 50 grams/
      300 meters
Size 4 (3.5 mm) 16" (40 cm) circular needle or size to
    obtain gauge
Size 6 (4 mm) straight or double pointed needles –
    Bind Off only
Marker

GAUGE
24 sts = 4" (10 cm) with size 6 (4 mm) needles in stockinette stitch

ABBREVIATIONS
P3tog: Purl 3 stitches together.

M1: Make one stitch – with left needle lift the running thread between the stitch just worked and the next stitch, from front to back, and knit into the back of the resulting loop.

BEGIN WITH THE BRIM

Cast on 160 (176) sts.

Place marker and join in the round, being careful not to twist stitches.

Round 1: Knit.

Round 2: Knit.

Round 3: P6, *P3tog, P13; repeat from * ending with P7 — 140 (154) sts.

Round 4: Purl.

Rounds 5 & 6: Knit.

Round 7: P5, *P3tog, P11; repeat from * ending with P6 — 120 (132) sts.

Round 8: Purl.

Rounds 9 & 10: Knit.

Round 11: P4, *P3tog, P9; repeat from * ending with P5 — 100 (110) sts.

Round 12: Purl.

Rounds 13 & 14: Knit.

Rounds 15 & 16: Purl.

Repeat rounds (13-16) 3 (4) more times.

The brim will be folded over when the hat is finished.

BODY

Knit 8 rounds.

Increase Round: *K25 (22), M1; repeat from * to end of round 104 (115) sts.

Knit every round until stockinette stitch section measures 4 (5)"/10 (13) cm.

TOP OF CROWN

Knit 2 rounds.

Purl 2 rounds.

Repeat last 4 rounds 4 more times.

Increase Round: *K26 (23), M1; repeat from * to end of round 108 (120) sts.

Knit 1 round.

Purl 2 rounds.

BIND OFF

Set-Up for 3-Needle Bind Off: With circular needle, K81 (90), leave these stitches on circular needle; with double pointed needle, knit the last 27 (30) sts of the round. With the same double pointed needle, remove marker and knit the first 27 (30) sts of the round. With a second double pointed needle, K54 (60).

You now have 54 (60) stitches for the Back of the hat on 1 double pointed needle, and the 54 (60) stitches for the Front of the hat on a second double pointed needle.

Use the 3-Needle Bind Off Method (see below) to Bind Off. Break the yarn and sew in end. Fold the brim over and sew in the end so that it doesn't show when folded over.

Alternately, if you wish you may bind off all the stitches for the hat; fold it in half and sew the Front and Back together.

3-NEEDLE BIND OFF

With stitches of Back of hat on 1 needle and stitches of Front on another, hold Front and Back together with Wrong Sides facing to make a ridged seam on the outside (right side) of the hat.

With another (3rd) LARGER sized needle:

1) Insert 3rd needle into first stitch on Front left needle and, without removing it, insert 3rd needle into first stitch on Back needle and knit these two stitches together.

2) Repeat once more.

3) There are 2 stitches on right needle, pass first stitch over second stitch and off end of needle (the same as a regular bind off).

Repeat steps 1 and 3 until all the stitches are bind off.

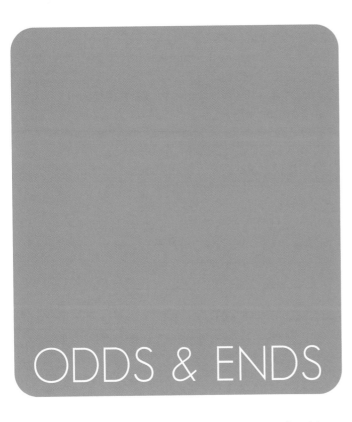

ODDS & ENDS

A little time, bits of leftover yarn and a lot of love is all it takes to create a warm gift for someone very special. This hat design is perfect for using all that yarn left from previous projects.

Design by: Deb Gemmell
Experience Level: Beginner

SIZES
Finished Circumference: 17 (18, 19)"

MATERIALS
DK, Light Worsted Weight Yarn
    Royal Blue (MC) 1.5 ounces/100 yards,
       45 grams/92 meters
    Lime Green small amount
Worsted weight yarns
    Yellow small amount
    Red small amount
Size 4 (3.5 mm) 16" (40 cm) circular needle or
    size to obtain gauge
6 markers

GAUGE
24 sts = 4" (10 cm)

STRIPE SEQUENCE
Using up all your bits and pieces of leftover yarn, work the following sequence, changing the color for each new set of rounds, using our model colors or as many colors as you wish.
Knit 2 rounds.
Knit 4 rounds.
Knit 1 round.
Knit 3 rounds.
Knit 1 round.

TO BEGIN
With MC and circular needle, cast on 96 (102, 108) sts. Place a marker and join in the round, being careful not to twist the stitches.
Knit every round for 1" (2.5 cm).
Increase Round: Slip marker, *K16 (17, 18), M1; repeat from * to end of round — 102 (108, 114) sts.
Purl 2 rounds.
Knit 1 round.
Knit in Stripe Sequence for 4 (4, 5)"/10 (10, 13) cm.

CROWN
With MC, knit every round for ½ (1, 1)"/1 (2.5, 2.5) cm.
Marker Round: With MC, slip marker, K17 (18, 19), *place marker, K17 (18, 19); repeat from * to end of round — 6 markers in place.
Decrease Round: *Slip marker, slip 1, K1, Psso, knit to next marker; repeat from * to end of round.
Repeat the last round until the stitches are stretched around the circular needle (somewhere around 54-60 sts on needle). Break the yarn leaving an 8" (20 cm) tail. Thread this tail through the remaining stitches on the needle, pull tightly and secure the tail on the inside of the hat.

FINISHING
Sew in the end of yarn from your cast on edge on the Right Side, so it will not be seen when the brim is rolled up.

ABOUT CABIN FEVER

Cabin Fever is a design company created by sisters Deb and Lynda Gemmell to feed their knitting habit. From an idea hatched on the deck of their cabin in Northern Ontario over several summers, Cabin Fever has grown into the largest independent knitting pattern publisher in Canada.

We welcome your comments and suggestions.
Please drop by, write, phone, fax or email us at:

Cabin Fever
Orillia, Ontario, Canada
Phone: 800-671-9112; 705-326-1900 (Canada)
Website: www.cabinfever.ca
Email: info@cabinfever.ca

YARNS USED IN MODELS

Faux Fur Fun – Page 6
Lion Brand Fun Fur, #209 Mango
Lion Brand Cotton-Ease, #133 Orangeade

Chameleon – Page 8
Lion Brand Fun Fur Prints, #231 Fireworks
Lion Brand Cotton-Ease, #133 Orangeade

Bernice's Tam – Page 10
Lion Brand Microspun, #148 Turquoise

Halton Crown Hat – Page 12
Lion Brand Microspun, #109 Royal Blue, #148 Turquoise,
#158 Buttercup, #194 Lime

Blue & White – Page 14
Lion Brand Cotton, #183 Periwinkle, #100 White

Here Kitty – Page 16
Lion Brand Microspun, #109 Royal Blue

Jumping Jacks – Page 20
Lion Brand baby soft, #102 Aqua
Lion Brand Microspun, #153 Black

Little Flap-Cap – Page 23
Lion Brand Wool-Ease, #107 Blue Heather,
#112 Red Sprinkles, #157 Pastel Yellow

Candy Dots – Page 26
Lion Brand Cotton, #100 White, #183 Periwinkle,
#298 Sherbert Swirl

Cable Rib Hat – Page 28
Lion Brand Wool-Ease, #112 Red Sprinkles

Elf Swirl – Page 30
Lion Brand Magic Stripes, #200 Jelly Bean Stripe

Carousel – Page 32
Lion Brand Microspun, #109 Royal Blue, #158 Buttercup,
#113 Cherry Red

Lace Cowl – Page 34
Lion Brand Babysoft, #102 Aqua

Reversible Hat – Page 36
Lion Brand Wool-Ease, #112 Red Sprinkles

Ribbed Cap – Page 38
Lion Brand Wool-Ease, #107 Blue Heather, #157 Pastel Yellow

Waves – Page 40
Lion Brand Magic Stripes, #204 Bright Spring

Odds & Ends – Page 42
Lion Brand Fun Fur, Microspun, Cotton, Wool-Ease

KOOLER DESIGN STUDIO BOOKS **Produced By:**
Kooler Design Studio • 399 Taylor Blvd., Ste. 104
Pleasant Hill, CA 94523 • www.koolerdesign.com
Creative Director, Donna Kooler • Technical Editor, Marsha Hinkson
Graphic Designer/Illustrator, María Rodríguez
Proofreaders: Judy Swager, Karen Tam • Photo Stylist, Basha Kooler
Photographer, Dianne Woods

Published By:

the art of everyday living

ISBN 1-57486-654-0